THE ULTIMATE KIDS GUIDE TO SOCIAL MEDIA

HOW TO STAY SAFE, BUILD HEALTHY ONLINE HABITS & HAVE FUN!

Copyright ©2023 *Rebecca Telemaque*
All Rights Reserved

Table of Contents

Chapter 1: The Basics 1

Chapter 2: The Good vs. The Bad 5

Chapter 3: Safety Basics 11

Chapter 4: Let's Talk About Time 14

Chapter 5: Friends 24

Chapter 6: Enemies 27

Chapter 7: Posting 35

Chapter 8: Privacy 38

Chapter 9: Selfies, Videos, and More 43

Chapter 10: Online vs. Reality 46

Chapter 11: Stunts, Challenges, and Peer Pressure 54

Chapter 12: Rumours and Fake News 58

Chapter 13: Bullies and Trolls 63

Chapter 14: Reporting 66

Chapter 15: Working With Parents/Guardians To Stay Safe 69

Chapter 1: The Basics

This book was designed to teach you everything you need to know to stay safe (and have fun) online and on social media. There is a lot to learn, but no worries! We've got you covered! Before we dig in, let's review the basics.

What is the internet?

The internet is a special connection between millions of devices (like phones, tablets, computers, game systems, smart TVs, etc.) all over the world! It allows people to access information from other people and to share information from their devices.

What is social media?

Social media is a variety of different apps and websites that were designed to help people connect with each other online. They allow people to interact by creating and sharing different information, ideas, comments, photos, and videos over virtual networks.

Let's talk social media safety!

You might be wondering, what is social media safety, and why is it important? Well, kids are spending more and more time online and on social media. While this can be fun, educational, and a great way to keep in touch with friends, it is important that you know how to be safe and responsible. The best way to do this is by learning about potential dangers, appropriate use, and healthy online habits.

It is important that your parents/guardians are able to help you to develop good habits and make a clear plan with you about what is allowed, what's not allowed, and what to do if you have a problem. At the end of this book, you and your parents/guardians should sit down together and create a plan, so you both know exactly what the rules are. This plan is called a social media agreement, and we will talk about it in more detail later in the book.

What a social media agreement will help you and your family do

1. To keep your information private

2. To keep your relationships strong & respectful

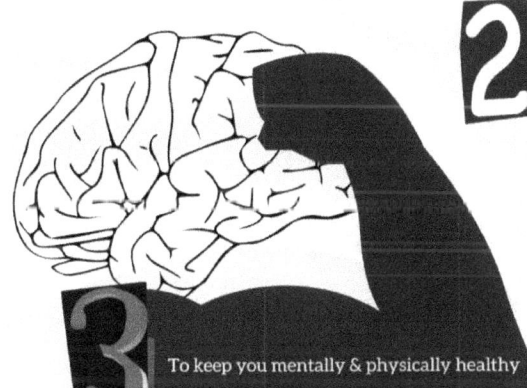
3. To keep you mentally & physically healthy

4. To make sure unsafe people **DO NOT** have access to you

5. So you will know what to do if you see something inappropraite

6. So you will know what to do if you or someone else needs help

DANGER DANGER DANGER
7. So you can recognize potential dangers
DANGER DANGER DANGER

When to get social media

Each family has different rules about when it is OK to get social media and what social media platforms are allowed. Always remember that your parents/guardians know you best and are the best people to make good decisions about what is safe and healthy for you. Before you sign up for social media, make sure that it is something you are allowed to do first.

Once you have permission, the next step is to decide which apps to sign up for. This can be exciting and confusing – there are *soooo* many to choose from! A general guideline when deciding what apps are right for you is to look at the minimum age for the app. If you are under that age, is it not recommended that you sign up. Many apps have kid-friendly versions that would be a safer place for you to get started. Other than that, consider what apps your family and friends use so that you have safe people to connect with.

Chapter 2: The Good vs. The Bad

Social media and internet use have many benefits and many potential problems. Here are a few pros and cons for you to consider:

 A New Type of Friendship

Many kids find that it is more comfortable to chat and find out about someone online than it is in person. Often, online connections can lead to a deeper understanding of people whom you may not have otherwise known much about. For example, if someone in your class at school is super shy, they may not tell you much about themselves, but online, they may post things that help you to learn what you have in common with them. This may lead to you being better friends with them in real life as well as online.

Another way it can strengthen relationships is by making it easier to stay in touch and up to date with what's happening with someone you may have otherwise not stayed in contact with. It can also be an easy way to reconnect with friends and acquaintances that you have lost touch with. A great example of this is reconnecting with a good friend who used to go to your school but moved away with their family.

 International Connections

Social media provides a quick, easy way to see what is happening all over the world. It can be a great way to see photos and know about important life events of friends and family that are living outside your local area. It is a quick, convenient and affordable way to stay connected with friends and family worldwide.

 **Learn New Things and Unleash Your Potential!**

Social networks allow kids to see informative videos, news clips, and different perspectives on any topic you can think of. Whether you are into sports, arts, academics, games, etc., there are many posts and videos that can both inspire you and teach you to develop your talent. Posts and videos can help you to gain new knowledge and techniques from experts and other aspiring kids. It can also help you to learn more about different cultures, beliefs, and other people's perspectives.

Helps You Express Your Identity

Creating a social media profile gives kids the opportunity to express themselves and their identities. It gives you an opportunity to learn and follow topics that you are interested in. This can help you to recognize how many others share your interests and offer you an opportunity to identify with part of a group. No matter what your thing is: sports, academics, crafts, animals, games, etc., there is TONS of information, videos, and photos online about it.

 Builds Confidence

Connecting to others with similar interests and developing skills can increase kids' confidence and self-esteem. Learning a new skill online, getting better at what you already like, or just showing off your talent (with your parents/guardians' permission) can help remind you how special, creative, and talented you are.

 Can be an Unhealthy Outlet

Often kids overshare personal information. Social media is not a good place to post information that could be sensitive or private. Even private messages can sometimes be shared or accessed by other people. Once you post something, other people can leave comments, and they may not always say something that is nice or helpful.

Can be Addicting

Many kids have trouble limiting their time online and their social media use. When social media is used too often, it can become addicting and start to take away from other activities, interests, and school work. Online gaming and other time spent online can also have negative consequences.

Imposters

Who is that person? Social media can bring unwanted attention from strangers. It can bring people with bad intentions and scammers. Sometimes, criminals or other people with bad intentions will even pretend to be someone they are not online.

Inappropriate Content

Inappropriate content can sometimes come up on social media. Some kids make the mistake of posting inappropriate content which can never be fully erased (even if they delete the post or message later). Other kids come across inappropriate content by accident or sometimes can be sent inappropriate content by a friend or online contact.

Cyberbullies and Trolls

Just like in real life, there are some people who are just plain mean. Unfortunately, many people online feel that they can be unkind and threatening to others. These cyberbullies and trolls send messages and threats, make mean comments, and dislike others' statuses to try to scare them or make them feel bad.

 Can Hurt Your Confidence

Many people start to compare themselves with others online. This can be a problem because people don't usually post bad things about their life on social media, only the good ones. People's lives usually seem much better online than they are in person. If you start comparing yourself, your confidence could be hurt because you see the good and bad in your life but only the good in other people. Other kids can become very obsessed with getting likes and comments or a huge number of friends or followers.

There are lots of good things, and lots of bad things about social media (and the internet in general). By reading this book you will learn how to minimize the negatives, and have the best possible online experience.

Chapter 3: Safety Basics

Working To Stay Safe

Your parents'/guardians' job is to keep you safe. No matter how smart of a kid you are, sometimes you will miss things. Most adults will be able to notice warning signs that something might be unsafe that you may not be able to recognize. It is important that parents and guardians monitor what you are doing online so they can spot any dangers that you may have missed.

Parents/guardians have different ways to check up on their kids. Some may do regular device checks where they look to make sure everything is OK. Others may decide to install a monitoring app where they will get alerts if something may be wrong. Some parents/guardians will control the settings on their child's phone by connecting it to their phone. Many parents will choose a combination of these ways or create a way of their own that works well for them.

When your parents decide to allow you to use social media, it is important that you understand and follow the rules that they give you. Not only do they love you A LOT, but they also know you better than anyone else in the world and know what rules will work best. The best way to be clear about the rules is to create something called a social media safety agreement, which is basically an agreement about what is allowed, what is not allowed, what to do if you need help, and what happens if the rules are broken.

At the end of this book, you and your family can create a social media agreement. On the next page, there are some things that you and your parents/guardians may want to include in it.

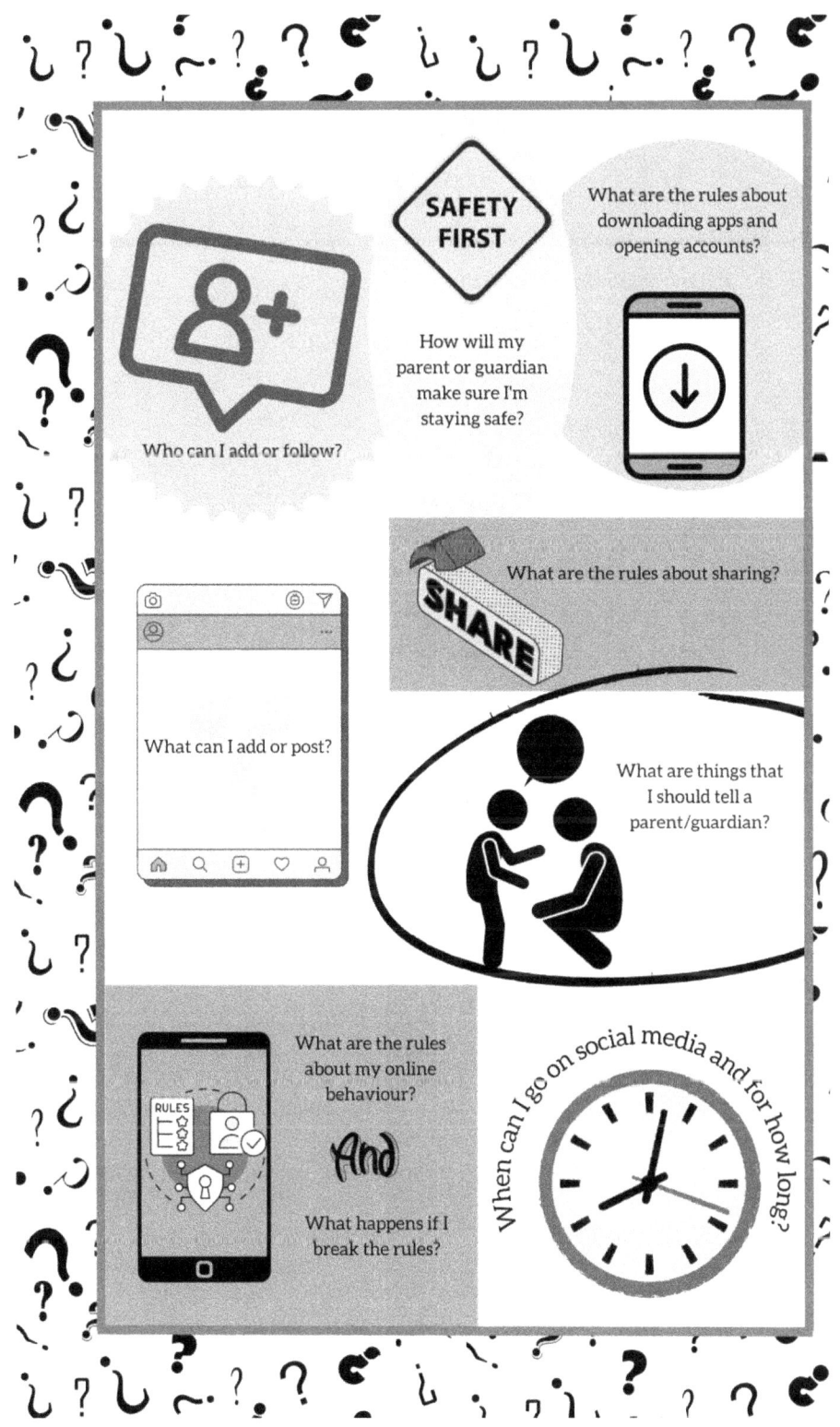

Chapter 4: Let's Talk About Time

Time Spent Online

Social media, the internet, and online games can all be fun, *BUT* there are some times when it's just not cool to use them. In fact, there are many times when using it would actually be very rude. So, when is social media use inappropriate or impolite?

> Here is a list of some times that it would usually be inappropriate or rude to use it:
> - During school
> - At the dinner table
> - During a conversation
> - At an event/presentation
> - Right before bed
> - During a religious service
> - When your parent/guardian or other adult who is responsible for you (like a teacher, coach or babysitter) said NO

Online Addictions

What a lot of people don't realize is that social media applications are actually businesses that are designed to make money. The more people they can get to sign up, and the more time they can get these people to spend on their app, the more money they make. This is because they make their money from other companies that pay them to advertise to their users. The more people they have on their applications and the more time those people spend there, the more they can get paid to advertise to them. For this reason, social media companies hire lots of people who specialize in designing their applications in a way that can be very addictive.

As you use social media apps, the companies that run the apps pay very close attention to everything you do on them. They keep data that tracks how much time you look at each photo, post, and video, who you contact the most, and what you have liked and commented on. As they do this, they learn about your likes and online habits.

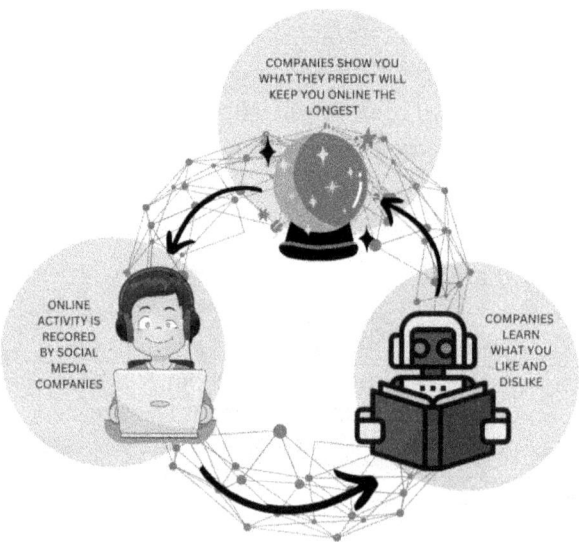

As these social media companies collect information about you, they are able to learn what you like and what you find interesting. When they know this, they begin to show you more things you will enjoy to get you to stay online longer. This is called an algorithm. It is how they decide what you see on their platforms (we will talk more about algorithms later in the book). The more time online you spend, the better the algorithm is able to predict what you will enjoy.

Another way they can try to tempt people to spend more time online is through alerts and notifications. This is when the social media platform or online game sends you messages and alerts to try to tempt you to come back online. For example, it may send you a message saying someone just beat your high score in a game, or that your friend just came online, or that someone just posted a new photo. These messages are designed to make you want to go back online to see what is happening.

All of this can make social media very addicting. While it can be lots of fun, it is important to keep track of how much time you spend online. Experts recommend that kids have no more than 2 hours of screen time a day, including social media, TV, and video games. It is a very smart idea to try to limit yourself to staying in this timeframe. Also, whenever you get an app, it is smart to turn off the notifications and alerts. This way, it will be harder for social media companies to trick you into spending more time on their apps than you should. It is also important to understand and recognize some of the warning signs that you may be developing an addiction to social media, online gaming, or the internet.

WARNING SIGNS

There are many things that can show you that you may be spending too much time online or even be developing an addiction. Here are a few warning signs to watch out for.

Excessive Online Gaming

Feeling like you need to beat your last score or hit a goal in the game no matter how long it takes, how tired you are or what else you had planned to do.

Constant Checking

Checking likes, comments, and views more and more often.

FOMO (Fear of Missing Out)

Always wanting to see every post, snap, or reel that your contacts have posted and being afraid you will miss one.

Snap Streaks

Needing to send them at specific times no matter what.

Excessive Online Spending

Usually, this one applies more to older people, but some kids have spent more than they should online. You should never spend any money online without the permission of a parent or guardian.

It Takes Up All Your Time

Spending a lot of time online each day - even when you know you should be sleeping or doing something else.

Your Relationships Started to Suck

It negatively impacts your other relationships and activities. Maybe you see friends less often, or they are annoyed that you are always on your device.

It Consumes Your Thoughts

While everyone thinks about social media or the internet sometimes, if you think about it almost all the time when you are not using it, that's a warning sign. Another one is if you start to avoid other activities to go online. This may look like you no longer want to play your favorite sport, hang out with your friends in person, or do some other activity that you used to love because you would rather be online.

You Use it to Cope

If you start to use it as a way to deal with or hide your sadness, anger, loneliness, or other negative emotions.

You Become a Gump

You get upset or irritated when you can't use it.

If you notice some of these signs, it is important to talk to an adult. The earlier you notice that there may be a problem, the easier it is for them to help you fix it. There are many different ways they can help you do this. They may start a new social media agreement with you that includes new rules to help you make more healthy choices, they may help you to find other things that you enjoy doing instead, or in some cases, you may need to speak to a counsellor to give you some extra help.

Chapter 5: Friends

Adding Friends

On social media, being "friends" can be a bit different than being friends in real life. Often, people online will friend request or follow celebrities, strangers, people they don't know very well, or sometimes even people they don't really like!

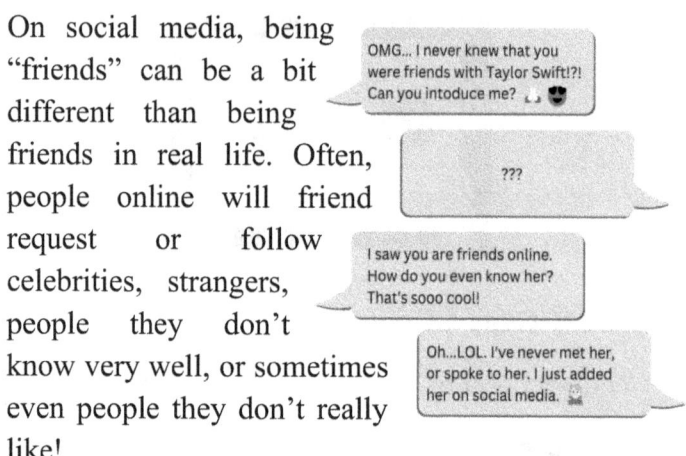

This can be surprising, exciting, scary, and dangerous. It is important to understand who is usually safe to be connected to, who may be unsafe to be connected to, and what the rules are in your family about connecting with people online. Keep in mind what people are usually safe and what people are possibly unsafe, and think about this when making your social media agreement with your family.

On the next page there is a guideline to give you some ideas about who is usually safe and who may be unsafe. Be sure to follow the rules in your family. If you're unsure if it is OK, ask a parent or guardian for their opinion before you consider adding the person as a friend or following them.

Usually Safe to Friend

- Your BFF or another friend you know in person
- Kids you know from your school
- A family member like your grandparents, cousins, aunts, uncles, etc.
- A friend from an extracurricular activity
- Someone you and your parents know in person that is about your age. For example, a child that you play with at the park, someone that you play with on your street or your parents/guardian friend's kids.

May be Unsafe

- Someone you never met in real life
- Someone who says they know you or your friend but that you don't remember
- Someone your parents/guardians don't approve of
- Someone you know but that is often unkind or makes you uncomfortable
- Someone who says you won something or offers to buy you something or give you a gift
- Someone who is much older than you

Remember, if you notice something strange about one of your friends online, TELL YOUR PARENTS/GUARDIANS!!! The internet is a weird place, and sometimes our friends can make poor online choices or may be struggling and need help. Other times an unsafe person may pretend to be someone they are not and may even pretend to be one of your friends! Either way, an adult can help. If something feels wrong or weird, it probably is. Trust your gut feeling!

Chapter 6: Enemies

Scammers

There are different types of scammers. They all have different ways of getting what they are looking for. Take a look at the list below of things that scammers may be trying to do.

- To steal online belongings in your games
- To access online gift cards, credit cards, or banking information
- To access your social media account
- To trick you into believing that they are someone your age
- To become your friend in order to trick, bully or pressure you into doing things you want to do later

So how do you know if someone may be a scammer? Well, it can be pretty hard to tell, but take a look at this list of warning signs.

WARNING

- They ask personal questions
- They ask you to give them online gifts (like points or belongings in games)
- They ask to meet you or want to know your address or where you go to school
- They ask for one of your passwords
- They ask for numbers on a gift card you have or for a credit card or banking information
- They ask for photos or videos of you that make you uncomfortable
- They ask you to keep something a secret, or they threaten or blame you for things
- They don't want your parents/guardians to know you are talking to them
- They know things about you that you don't remember telling them
- They ask questions or say things that make you feel uncomfortable or that you feel are inappropriate
- They show you things or tell you things that you know are inappropriate or that make you uncomfortable

If you see any of these warning signs, talk to your parent or guardian to see what they think. It may be a scammer, or it may just be another kid with bad manners. It's always smart to check with a safe adult. Remember to always be careful and stick to talking to and playing with people you know in real life. No matter how smart you are, you won't always be able to recognize a scammer or unsafe person. Some scammers are so good at what they do that even super-smart adults get tricked by them!

So, you are probably wondering… what happens if I do meet a scammer? Then what should I do? Well, the most important thing is to NEVER give them any information about yourself. Next, you should tell a parent or guardian. This is especially important if someone has made you feel unsafe or done something that made you uncomfortable. Most of the time, you or your parent/guardian can block, delete and unfriend the person, so they no longer have access to you. You can also report the person to the social media site you are using to help keep others safe. In some very serious cases, your parent/guardian may need to file a police report.

NOOOO!!!! The parents are gonna ruin my plans!!!

Filters and Deep Fakes

Filters are a type of photo-altering technology that can make someone look different. Some are designed to make someone's skin look smoother or get rid of pimples, others change the way you look completely, and some add in fun elements to a photo. Many kids (and adults) use filters for fun. My personal favorite is a filter that makes you look like a dog. LOL.

This can be fun to play with, but it is important to keep in mind that it is not real. Many of the photos you see online of people looking perfect are actually of the person using a photo filter. This is why you should never compare the way you look to the way someone looks online. Chances are, if someone looks totally flawless, the way they look in their online photo is probably thanks to a filter and is usually different from how they look in real life.

There is another type of technology that changes the way people look. It is called Deep Fake Technology. It is kind of like a filter, except it can make a person look and sound exactly like someone else. For example, if someone is tech-savvy and has a sample of my voice and a few photos of me, they can use this technology to make a video or do a video call pretending to be me. Often these videos are so realistic that they trick the closest friends and family of the person they are pretending to be. Sometimes only experts with other special technology can tell the difference between a real person and someone using deep fake technology!

Grooming

(Not this type of groomer)

When most kids hear someone say grooming, they think about taking their dog or cat to the groomer to get a bath and a hair and nail cut. That is one type of grooming, but there is also another meaning for the word that not many kids know about. Grooming can also mean a technique that unsafe people use to trick or trap someone so that it is easier to force them to do something that they don't want to do.

So, you're probably wondering how do they do that? Well, they can be very sneaky. Usually, they start off being very nice, they learn a lot about you, sometimes they might give you things and be an amazing friend. Then once they know a lot about you, and maybe some of your secrets, they use that to try to get you to do things you don't want to. They usually start with things you only kind of don't want to do but then, over time, make you do things that are more and more dangerous and inappropriate, and that make you feel worse and worse.

Groomers can be hard to recognize, but check out the next page for some warning signs to look out for.

- They pretend to be very similar to you and be a very good friend (it might be hard to tell they are pretending!)
- They try to find out secrets about you (especially ones that could get you in trouble). Then use them against you later.
- They try to make you keep things secret from your parents/guardians.
- They make you do things that are uncomfortable (starting with things that are just a little uncomfortable and then that are more and more uncomfortable).
- They show you inappropriate things (starting with things that are a little inappropriate and over time, things that get more inappropriate).
- They encourage you to break the rules.
- They bully or threaten you.
- They try to convince you that you will be in trouble if you tell.
- They tell you things that confuse you.
- They try to make you believe that your friends and parents don't love you or understand you (this is a lie, I promise, you are VERY special and VERY loved!).
- They try to talk with you secretly.
- They buy you gifts, and then they say you owe them.

No matter how smart you are, it is still possible to be tricked by someone, especially someone older than you. Most kids are shocked, scared, embarrassed, and confused when they realize that something is wrong. It can be very hard to find out that someone who you thought was a friend had bad intentions all along, or in some cases, that they were a totally different person.

If you gave someone information or photos or videos of yourself that you know you shouldn't have, it is important to get help. If you were tricked or threatened into doing something inappropriate, it is important to get help. It is normal to be scared, overwhelmed, confused and have a lot of big feelings. A trusted adult can help you to stay safe and deal with those difficult feelings.

Even if you are being threatened, an adult can keep you and those around you safe. If you are too scared to tell a parent/guardian, you can tell another adult that makes you feel safe, like a teacher, a coach, a counsellor, an adult family member, or a friend's parent.

Chapter 7: Posting

Posting and Sharing

What things are OK to post or share? Before you think about posting or sharing anything, be sure that you discuss with your parents/guardians what the rules are for you. Some families decide that there is a no posting rule in their house, while other families may allow posting with permission for each post, and other families will allow posting certain things. If you are allowed to post, it is best to stick to things that are not too personal. There are some things that you should NEVER post. Take a look at a list of them below.

Is it OK to Post This?

Before you decide to post anything online, you should always take a few minutes to consider if it is a good idea. Here are some questions you can ask yourself that will help you to decide if it is a good idea:

- Is this kind?
- Is this true?
- Could someone else find this upsetting or embarrassing?
- Does this give out personal information about myself or someone else?
- Is this appropriate?
- Am I allowed to post this?
- Is there anyone I wouldn't want to see this?

Can You Delete It?

If you do make a mistake and post something that you regret, you can try to delete it. Most social media apps have the option to take down a photo, video, post, or comment. BUT the thing with the internet is that even once you delete something, it never fully disappears. Once you post something, it's out there somewhere forever!

Even if you delete something and you can't see it anymore, that doesn't mean it's fully gone. People often take photos of posts and messages that they can later look at again or share with other people. Even if you delete your post, any photos or screenshots that people took of what you posted can still be viewed, shared, or posted on someone else's account. Also, many people who are very tech-savvy can still find deleted posts and messages. The internet and social media companies always keep hidden copies of photos, posts, and messages… FOREVER. Anyone with the right set of skills can still access things that have been deleted at any time in the future. Before you post something, always consider if there could be any reason that you may not want someone to see it. If there is any possibility that it may be something you will regret, DON'T POST IT!

NFL MVP's deleted post from 15 years ago

Chapter 8: Privacy

Passwords

Any time you set up a social media account, you will need to make a password. Your password should be something that is easy for you to remember but something that is hard for other people to guess.

Once you make your password make sure to tell your parent/guardian and NO ONE ELSE. It can sometimes be tempting to share your password with your BFF, a sibling, or someone else that you care about. This is NOT a good idea. It is also important to always be aware of who can see you entering your password. Make sure you are somewhere private, out of everyone's eyesight, when you type in your password.

If someone has your password, they can see everything on your account or even make posts pretending to be you. No one ever wants to believe that someone they care about would use their account to do something inappropriate, but unfortunately, it happens a lot more than you would think! The problem is that because it is your account, you are the one who is responsible for how it is used (even if they used your password and did something on there that you knew nothing about).

Hackers

Hacking is when someone other than you is able to access your accounts. Most often, this is done by someone who knows your password or who is able to guess what your password is. Once they are into your account, they can post ANYTHING on your account pretending to be you. They can even message anyone from your account pretending to be you. Also, they can also see EVERYTHING you have done on the account, including reading any personal messages you have sent to any of your contacts.

This can be a BIG problem. What they say and post could be something inappropriate that you get you in trouble or embarrass you. Sadly, this type of hacking is most commonly done by a friend or someone you know. This usually happens when they are angry with you about something and don't think ahead about your feelings or the other possible consequences.

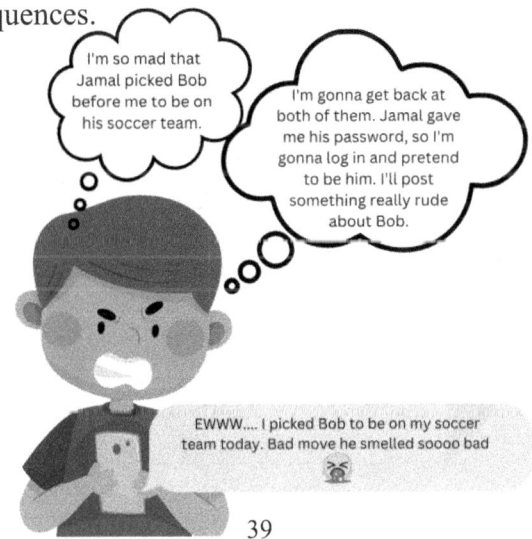

The good news is that this type of hacking is easy to prevent. By keeping your password private (except telling your parent or guardian) and making it something that is not easy to guess, it is very unlikely that you would be a victim of this type of hacking.

The other type of hacking is done by people who are very knowledgeable about technology. Some of them will try to gain access to other people's devices and account just to see if they are smart enough to do it (it's kind of like a challenge to them). Some hackers will try to gain access to the accounts of organizations, governments, or famous people to find out and share information that is supposed to be private.

The last type of hackers are criminals who try to get access to other people's accounts to commit crimes. There can be many ways they can do this. The one way they can do this is called fishing (No, not like the kind you do with a fishing rod). Online fishing is when a criminal tries to trick someone into giving them personal information like passwords or banking information.

Example

You receive a message saying that someone just changed the password for your social media account. Then it says, "If you didn't make this change click this link and enter your old password." A lot of people will panic and think, "I didn't just change my password!" They will click the link and enter their password. The trick is that no one actually changed the password. The purpose of the email was to trick you into clicking a link and entering what your actual password is. This way, the hacker can now access your account.

Anytime you receive a message or email asking for a password or for money, be very careful. Usually, this is a hacker trying to gain access to your account, your gift card balances, or to banking or credit card information. Never give out this information without checking with a parent or guardian first and having them make sure that you are not being scammed by a hacker.

Chapter 9: Selfies, Videos, and More

Photos and Videos

Seeing photos and videos of your friends and of celebrities online can be lots of fun! When used responsibly, social media is a great way to see fun and interesting things that people are doing. Some videos can even teach you how to do new, creative and cool things! Lots of people use social media to see photos of their friends and family and watch videos that are funny, entertaining, or educational. However, there are some photos and videos online that are inappropriate such as those with violence, bad language or nudity.

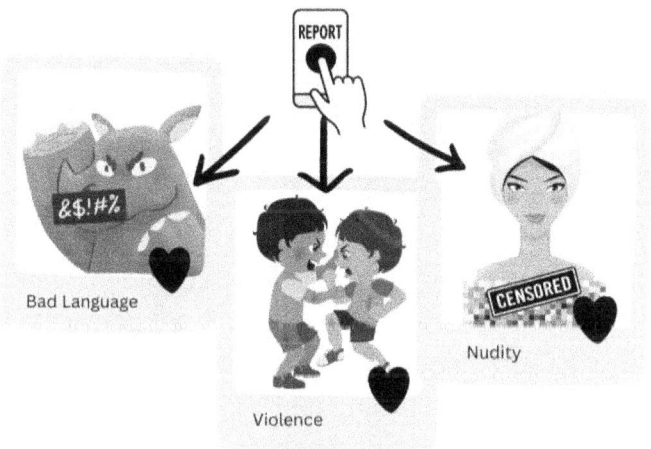

If you accidentally see something that you feel is inappropriate, tell a parent or guardian what you saw.

Report the photo or video to the social media platform so they can review it and see if it should be removed. If the photo or video is of someone you know personally, make sure you get an adult's help right away to make sure they can keep the person safe.

If you are allowed to post photos or videos, never take or send any photo or video of you or anyone else without clothing or doing something dangerous or violent. Also, if you use any type of video chat, beware of what you are doing while you are on the call.

For example, if you are on a video call with your BFF while you are getting ready for bed, before you change into your PJs, turn off the call. Even if you are comfortable changing in front of your BFF in real life, you should never do it on a video call. This is because sometimes a photo could be taken of you without clothing while you are on the call, or it is possible that someone else could hack into the call and see you changing on video. It's also possible that your BFF may not be in a private place. How would you feel if their parent or sibling walked past their device and saw you changing?

Consequences of Inappropriate Photos or Videos

Thought bubbles: "OMG!!! I didn't wanna see that! Why were they doing that? It was so wierd..." "I should tell my Dad."

When kids see or are a part of inappropriate photos and videos, there can be lots of different outcomes. A lot of different feelings can come up, such as embarrassment, confusion, or sadness about what they saw or were a part of. Sometimes they may worry about what other people will think of them for seeing or being in the photo or video. In more extreme cases, kids may start to feel depressed or have a lot of anxiety. If you find yourself in this situation, speak to a trusted adult about what happened.

Remember, if you decide to take or post an inappropriate photo or video, there are possible consequences. There can be consequences at home from parents or guardians, at school, or for older people at work. Depending on what is shown in the photo or video, there can even be legal consequences from the police for taking or sharing a photo or video that is inappropriate.

Chapter 10: Online vs. Reality

What are the differences between online and reality? Well, there are actually a lot! Remember earlier in the book when we started talking about an algorithm? (The social media companies' way of deciding what to show you on their platforms so that you stay as interested as possible). Well, algorithms can be great because they help us to the see things that we are most interested in and things that are based on topics that we really enjoy. Algorithms are one of the reasons people have so much fun online!

However, algorithms also mean that everyone sees different things because it is designed to show you things you will like and agree with. In the real world, you will see things you like and that you don't like. Every day, you will be exposed to ideas you agree with, ideas you disagree with, and new ideas that you haven't thought of before.

For example, if you have spent a lot of time watching cute and funny cat videos and liked a lot of them, the algorithm will show you more cat videos. Then if you ask google, "What is better, cats or dogs?" because the algorithm knows that you prefer cats, it will show you what it thinks you want to see – lots of other people who also think cats are the best! BUT, if instead of cats, you always liked cute and funny dog videos, then the algorithm would show you things about why dogs are amazing. In real life, if you ask a bunch of people, "What's better, cats or dogs?" you would find people that would give you reasons that cats are amazing, people who would give you reasons they like dogs best, people who like both, and people who don't really like either.

It is important to remember that everyone sees different things online based on their likes and dislikes. Social media and other internet companies, such as Google, are designed to show you things you like and agree with (because nobody likes to be wrong). By doing this, they hope that you will spend more time online so that they can make more money. This is important to remember because no one is always right. It is important that we are able to hear other people's points of view and recognize that there are people who think differently from us. That is part of what makes the world so beautiful and interesting!

There is also another way that online is very different from reality. In real life, people have both good and bad moments, they have fun and boring moments, and they have successes and failures. Life is full of all sorts of different feelings and experiences, and everybody has some that are positive and some that are negative. The problem is that our online life usually only shows the good ones.

Think about it, if you are having a horrible hair day, all your favorite clothes are in the laundry, and you are wearing the oldest, ugliest shirt you have that is actually a bit too small and stained, and you have a pimple on your nose that's so big you look like Rudolph (the red nose reindeer) chances are you are not going to take a selfie to post that day. BUT the day you wake up with your skin looking flawless and glowing, your hair is doing exactly what it is supposed to do, and you have a super cool new outfit on, chances are you will be feeling pretty good about the way you look, and you might even take a selfie to post.

Here's the thing, everyone has both types of days. BUT, when you look at your own life and compare it to someone else's online life, you are not seeing what their life is actually like. You are comparing a list of their best moments to your good and bad moments. Always remember, if you look at someone else's profile, you are not seeing the full picture of what their life is actually like. You only see what they decide that they want you to see.

Something else to keep in mind that is kind of weird is that some people post fake things online to make their life look more perfect and interesting. Many of the flawless photos you see and not actually that flawless. Often the person has used a filter (a special type of photo-altering technology) to make their photos look perfect. Sometimes, people also make posts that are not entirely true. Take a look at some of the funny examples on the next page.

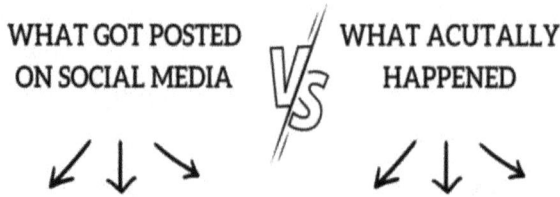

Remember, there are lots of differences between online and reality. Take a look at the lists below and compare the differences.

ONLINE

- People with beauty filters
- Their biggest accomplishments
- Things that may not be true
- Fun with friends
- The most fun and interesting things they did

REAL LIFE

- Bad things and good things
- Fun moments, boring moments, sad moments, angry moments, etc.
- Great accomplishments and huge failures
- Fun with friends and disagreements with friends
- Days where you look flawless and bad hair days, and days with pimples.

Self Esteem and Self Image

So, you might be wondering, what is the big deal about things being different online than in real life? Why is it important to understand that people can fake things online? Well, it can feel pretty crappy if you compare your life to what parts of someone's life you see online. If you believe that everyone you see online looks flawless all the time, only does fun things, and is successful in everything they do, it can cause a lot of problems.

A lot of people compare themselves to others online but forget to consider that someone's online version of their life is very different than their actual life. When kids compare themselves to other kids' online versions of their life, it can damage their self-confidence and cause low self-esteem, poor self-image, negative body image, and sometimes even eating disorders or depression.

Social media and other things that kids see online can make them feel way more insecure than things they see in real life. In some cases, it makes kids feel obligated to post untrue things to feel more interesting or can make them feel obligated to post things that may be inappropriate in order to get more attention. If you notice that you are feeling any of these things, it is important to speak to a trusted adult so they can help you to manage these feelings.

Chapter 11: Stunts, Challenges, and Peer Pressure

Some online challenges may be fun or motivating, but others may be gross, inappropriate, stupid, or dangerous. For example, if you and your friends have a challenge to see who can draw the best picture and post it or who can do the longest handstand, as long as you are allowed to post, it could be fun. BUT, if someone challenges you to send a video of you licking a toilet, shaving your head, eating soap, or doing something else that is either gross, embarrassing, inappropriate, or dangerous, **IT'S A VERY BAD IDEA…. DON'T DO IT!!!**

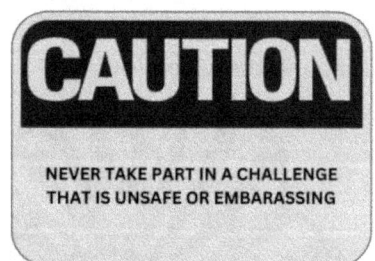

NEVER TAKE PART IN A CHALLENGE THAT IS UNSAFE OR EMBARASSING

While most of the bad challenges would come with consequences at home and sometimes at school, some of the really bad challenges can have legal consequences from the police. Remember, what you post online NEVER fully goes away (even if you delete it)! It's always smart to get permission from your parent or guardian before participating in any online challenge.

How To Cope With Online Peer Pressure

You have probably heard about peer pressure before. It is when you feel pressured to do something that other people are doing even though it may not be something you really want to do, or it may make you uncomfortable. In some cases, peer pressure can be a good thing. For example, if all of your friends take school very seriously and pressure you to study for an upcoming test or review, is positive peer pressure. You may not really want to study, but having them encourage you to do it could be a good thing. Another example is if you a part of a team sport or activity and your friends encourage you to practice with them so you can get better. That could also be a good form of peer pressure because it can help you get better at something you enjoy. However, there are times when our friends can pressure us to do things that are not a good idea. This can happen both in person and online.

Here are a couple of questions for you to think about.

1. What type of peer pressure do you think you might come across online?
2. What are some ways you can deal with it and make sure that you make wise choices?

It is always a good idea to have a plan about how you can respond if you feel you are being peer pressured to do something that you know is wrong or that makes you uncomfortable. Planning in advance how to deal with it will help you to be prepared to make a good decision about how to respond, as you will not be caught off guard and left to think of a solution on the spot.

The best way to deal with peer pressure is to try to avoid the negative kind as much as possible. Although it is never possible to fully avoid it, limiting yourself to online friends and contacts who have similar beliefs and moral values to you will help. People who think like you are less likely to try to get you to do things that make you uncomfortable or that you know are a bad idea.

If you are feeling pressured, let the person or people know how they are making you feel and ask them to stop. If it continues, and if you are comfortable, you can tell the person directly, "I have asked you to stop, and you're not respecting me, so I'm going offline now." If it feels too scary to tell them directly, you can just say, "I have to go now." and then log off. Once you have logged off, talk to a trusted adult about what happened. They will be able to listen to your concerns and help you come up with a plan.

Chapter 12: Rumours and Fake News

A rumour is information about somebody that may or may not be true. Often, it is an untrue story about somebody that was made up to damage the person's reputation, damage their relationships, and to make them feel hurt. Sometimes rumours are known and spread by just a few people. Other times, they are known and spread by many people.

Online rumours tend to spread much more quickly than they do in person. One person can make a post that can be seen instantly by hundreds or sometimes even thousands of people. Those people can then repost or share that information with all of their contacts, and their contacts can then share it with all of their contacts, and so on.

Part of being responsible online is avoiding any involvement in rumours. You should never say or spread any photos or information about someone else online that they may not like. People who start rumours or spread them online can face negative consequences at home, at school, at work (if they are older), and from the police. Often, if someone is known for spreading rumours they can lose other people's trust and often lose friends.

Someone who has been the victim of a rumour can be really impacted. Often, they feel hurt, sad, angry, and sometimes depressed. Many kids who have been the victim of a rumour worry that they may lose friends or have their reputations damaged. Sometimes they worry so much that they have trouble staying focused on school or getting things done. Other times the person is so upset that they try to get back at the person or people who spread the rumour (this is a very bad idea).

So, what should you do about it? If someone is spreading rumours about you online, seek help from a trusted adult to help you find the best way to deal with the situation. If you have been a part of an online rumour, or just said something that hurt someone's feelings, always apologize. Then, try to correct your mistake by deleting what you can, and making better decisions in the future.

Fake News

Fake news is when false information is disguised as news. It can be created as a joke or created to mislead people into believing something that is not true. It can sometimes be difficult to tell the difference between fake news and real news.

Sometimes people spread fake news accidentally. They can see something online and believe that it is true when it is actually untrue. Other times people or organizations can intentionally spread information that they know is untrue. There can be many different reasons for them to do this, such as to trick people, to try to make a joke, to make money, or to make people form a certain opinion about someone or something.

Fake news can be hard to spot, but there are a few signs you can look for to help you tell that it may be fake. Check them out on the next page.

Chapter 13: Bullies and Trolls

Online, just like in real life, it is possible to meet people who are bullies. Online bullying is called cyberbullying. It is when someone uses online messaging, video calls, posts, comments, or other communication over technology to harass, threaten or embarrass someone. Sometimes the bully is someone you know, and sometimes it can be a stranger. Other times a bully can make a fake account or pretend to be someone else so that you don't know who the bully is.

There is another type of online bully who is called a troll. A troll is someone who purposely tries to upset people and cause trouble online by making rude or offensive comments on people's social media posts. Often, they do this to many different people, including people they don't even know.

Bullying can have bad outcomes for both the person who is doing the bullying and the person who is being bullied. Take a look at the lists below of some things people can experience if they have been bullies or have been victims of bullying.

For the bully:

- Loss of respect and trust from friends, family, and acquaintances
- Negative impact on relationships
- Consequences at home, at school, at work for older people, and sometimes from the police
- Possible revenge from the victim or others
- Builds abusive patterns in relationships (this means it can be hard to stop bullying even once you're a grown up)

For the victim:

- Feelings of sadness, embarrassment, confusion, anger, loneliness, anxiety, and depression
- Loss of self-confidence and self-esteem
- Fear
- Acting out/getting revenge/violence
- Trouble keeping up with schoolwork

How should I deal with an online bully? Well, it depends on how serious it is. For example, if someone you are usually good friends with says something that is not very nice, you may feel comfortable enough to tell them to stop and let them know how it made you feel. On the other hand, if it is something that happens more than once, is from someone you don't know, or if it is something you find very upsetting, embarrassing or scary, then you need to speak to a trusted adult to help you plan your next steps. It is also a good idea to report the person to the social media platform that they are bullying on. This way, the social media company can investigate as well.

Chapter 14: Reporting

Before you start to use any new social media platform, you and your parent/guardian should sit down together and figure out how to report anything unsafe or inappropriate. There is a place on every social media app to report these types of things. When a report is filed, a safe adult will review the report, and they will decide what they need to do with that information. When something happens that you feel you need to report, you should always tell a parent/guardian or other trusted adult. If you see something where someone is in immediate or serious danger, you can call 911.

When it comes to reporting, the first thing you need to know is what can be reported. Here is a list of some things that you can report if you come across them online:

- Any type of bullying
- Inappropriate photos or videos
- Inappropriate language
- Requests for money or credit card info
- Requests for personal information or passwords
- Fake news and rumors
- Scams
- Someone pretending to be someone they're not
- Someone who asks for your location and schedule or tries to get you to meet them
- Someone doing something dangerous or hurting someone
- Anyone or anything that makes you feel unsafe

If in doubt... report it! When you report something, an adult will look things over to see if something is happening that is unsafe. They will be able to make a decision about what the best next steps are to take. It is better to report something that does not need to be reported than it is to ignore something that should be reported. The adult that gets the report will know if it is something that they need to take action for.

Chapter 15: Working With Parents/Guardians To Stay Safe

Parent and Guardian Monitoring

It is very important that parents or guardians monitor your online activity and social media to help keep you safe. After all, keeping you safe is one of their most important responsibilities! They can often see dangers that you may be unaware of. They may decide to do regular checks of your apps, messages, and photos to make sure everything is OK and that you are making safe, responsible, and healthy online choices. Lots of parents will also decide to install a monitoring app on your phone so that they will know right away if they are in danger of being mistreated online or making irresponsible choices.

Secret Codes

Sometimes it can be hard to tell a parent that you made a mistake or that you saw something uncomfortable or inappropriate. It can be hard to talk about it if something really scary happened online. Sometimes, you may feel like your parents/guardians need to know something but are unsure of how to actually say it.

One thing that a lot of families find helpful is to have a secret code. This can be a word, a phrase, or an emoji that you would never normally use. How it works is that you and your parents/guardians will know what this secret code is. If you send it to them or say it to them, it will tell them that it is time to do a device check to see what has been happening online. It will let them know that something happened that you need help with but that you are unsure of how to say it.

Social Media Agreement

Congratulations! You are now ready to sit down and make a Social Media Agreement with your family!

Everyone's social media agreement will look different. It is based on the rules you have in your family. A good social media agreement should be very detailed and set clear rules about what is and is not allowed. It should be written down. You and your parents or guardians should both sign it and have your own copy of it. If any rules change, then you should do an updated agreement so that you are always clear about what is expected of you. Many families like to be creative and make their own agreements, while other families prefer to fill out a premade version that they find available online.

If you and your family decide to create your own, it should include the following:

- When can I go on social media, and for how long?
- Who can I add or follow?
- What am I allowed to post?
- What are the rules about sharing?
- Am I allowed to spend money online? If so, how much?
- What are the rules about downloading social media apps and creating accounts?
- What are the rules about my online behaviour?
- How will my parents/guardians make sure I'm staying safe?
- What things should I tell my parents/guardians or another trusted adult?
- Are there any other rules or expectations in our family about my online activity?
- What happens if I break the rules?
- How often will we review and make changes to this agreement?

www.ingramcontent.com/pod-product-compliance
Lightning Source LLC
Chambersburg PA
CBHW071744040426
42446CB00012B/2467